First Writing Prompts

200 Just-Right Prompts That Motivate Young Learners to Write All Year Long!

by Pamela Chanko

New York • Toronto • London • Auckland • Sydney
Mexico City • New Delhi • Hong Kong • Buenos Aires

Teaching Resources

Cover design by Jorge J. Namerow
Interior design by BHG Graphic Design

ISBN-13: 978-0-545-23137-4 / ISBN-10: 0-545-23137-X

Copyright © 2010 by Pamela Chanko

Contents

Writing Prompts

Reproducibles for Student Writing

Introduction

I don't know what to write. This is a sentiment expressed by nearly every writer, from the youngest beginners to the most seasoned professionals. Even Ernest Hemingway, when asked about the most frightening thing he'd ever encountered, famously answered: "A blank sheet of paper."

But how about those who are just learning to write? In teaching young learners, the focus is usually on the act of writing itself: spelling, grammar, and often handwriting. But for many of these emergent writers, the most difficult part of the process is not the learning of mechanics—it's *just getting started.* Like Hemingway, many students may find the sight of an empty page far more frightening than even the toughest spelling test. Once they come up with an idea, however, they become engaged and are able to relax—and learn.

That's where *First Writing Prompts* comes in. These quick, simple ideas provide just the right push to get young students' pencils moving—along with their imaginations! In this book, you'll find engaging prompts on subjects that fit seamlessly with your curriculum all year long, from September's apples to June's class time capsules—and all the summer fun beyond. The prompts are organized by month, so it's easy to dip into the resource anytime and find a prompt that fits the season. But with 200 different prompts, you just might be tempted to choose one for every day of the year!

The prompts also provide students with opportunities to practice different forms of writing, including narrative, descriptive, expository, and persuasive. You'll find ideas to get students producing stories, friendly letters, blurbs, advertisements, directions, and more. In addition to sparking creative thinking, the prompts give students valuable practice for tests and assignments they'll encounter throughout their school years. While the ideas in this book are appealing and fun, make no mistake: they also pack plenty of academic punch, helping you to prepare students while meeting critical curriculum standards (see the box on page 6).

So, what's the secret to becoming a practiced writer? Any veteran author will tell you: sit down, grab that blank piece of paper, and *just write.* With *First Writing Prompts*, your students will never lack for a reason to do exactly that. You've got 200 just-right reasons right at your fingertips!

How to Use This Book

The quick and easy prompts in this resource are designed for maximum flexibility in your classroom, month by month around the year. In each section, you'll find prompts related to that month, including seasonal and holiday ideas as well as themes commonly taught at that time of year. Don't feel bound to use the book in order, though. There are also plenty of terrific "anytime" prompts throughout, so feel free to skip around! The following tips will give you an idea of the many ways to incorporate writing prompts into your curriculum. Just choose the ones that give you a perfect fit, and happy writing!

Before Writing

✱ Consider how often you'd like students to respond to prompts. For instance, you might post a "Prompt of the Day," a "Prompt of the Week," or simply provide writing prompts as options in the writing center.

✱ You can present the prompts to students in many different ways. They're short enough to copy on the board or chart paper for small-group or whole-class activities. For use in a center, you might photocopy the pages for the current month and allow students to choose any prompt they like. You can also make creativity "recipe cards" by copying each prompt on a separate card and storing the cards in a file box.

✱ Remember, the materials students use to write can play an important part in the process. By providing a nifty pencil-topper or a sheet of fun stationery, you can lure reluctant writers—and spark creativity. You'll find two different reproducible templates for student writing in the back of this book. The lined Write Around the Year sheet on page 47 can be used with prompts for every month. For prompts that include drawing (or anytime students want to add an illustration), use the Draw and Write template on page 48.

During Writing

✱ Writing prompts are a great resource for independent student journals. When students say they have nothing to write about, you always have an answer ready!

✱ The prompts make good seatwork, and they're also a way to ensure that "filler" activities have real value. Give a prompt to early finishers and you'll know they're using the time productively and creatively.

✱ Remember that writing doesn't always have to be a solo activity. The prompts can be used for shared writing experiences, small-group mini-lessons, and whole-class discussions as well.

✱ Of course, you can also use the prompts as homework assignments. If you're looking for a creative way to forge home-school connections, have parents work with children to respond to a prompt together.

After Writing

✳ Student writing can be presented in different ways. You might create a Writers' Wall and post students' best work, or have students create their own anthologies. You can also bind students' pieces into a class book.

✳ Encourage students to share their writing orally as well. You might have a regular "author reading" in which students read their work aloud and respond to classmates' questions and comments.

✳ Have students revisit their work on a regular basis to help ensure that they see writing as a process; even the very youngest writers should practice revising and editing to improve their work. This not only helps students track their own progress, but also helps them see that they don't have to get it "right" the first time. Writing is something that's supposed to change and grow—and often, the best writers spend most of their time rewriting. Once students internalize these concepts, they may never be frightened by a blank sheet of paper again!

Connections to the Language Arts Standards

The activities in this book are designed to support you in meeting the following standards for students in grades 1–3, outlined by Mid-continent Research for Education and Learning (McREL), an organization that collects and synthesizes national and state K–12 curriculum standards.

Uses the general skills and strategies of the writing process:

✳ Uses strategies to organize written work, such as including a beginning, middle, and ending and using a sequence of events

✳ Uses writing to describe familiar persons, places, objects, or experiences

✳ Writes in a variety of forms or genres, such as friendly letters, stories, poems, information pieces, invitations, personal experience narratives, messages, and responses to literature

✳ Writes for different purposes, such as to entertain, inform, explain, and communicate ideas

✳ Writes expository compositions; narrative accounts, such as poems and stories; autobiographical compositions; expressive compositions; responses to literature; and personal letters

Uses the stylistic and rhetorical aspects of writing:

✳ Uses descriptive words to convey ideas

✳ Uses language that clarifies and enhances ideas, such as figures of speech and sensory details

Source: *Content Knowledge: A Compendium of Standards and Benchmarks for K–12 Education*, 4th edition (Mid-continent Research for Education and Learning, 2004)

September

The Good, the Bad, and the Summer

What was the very best thing about your summer? What was the very worst thing? Explain why.

A School-Year Resolution

What do you most want to learn this year? Write a promise to learn it! Then tell how you will do it.

This Is the Way We'd Go to School

Pretend you could get to school any way you wanted, such as on a plane or riding on an animal. How would you go? Tell how it would be different from the way you get to school now.

How Do You Like Those Apples?

There are many ways to eat apples. You can eat them in applesauce or in an apple pie. Or you can just eat them plain. What do you think is the best way to eat apples? Give two reasons why.

A Few of My Favorite Things

Write a list of ten favorite things. Your list can include animals, foods, activities, or anything else that's important to you.

First Writing Prompts © 2010 by Pamela Chanko. Scholastic Teaching Resources

September

6

Cozy in the Classroom

Describe your favorite spot in the classroom. What does it look like? What do you do in this place? Tell why you like being there.

7

Way Up High in the Apple Tree

Pretend you are an apple. Write a story about your life on the tree. You can tell your color, name, and taste. You can also tell what happens after you get picked.

8

Follow Your Feelings

Finish each sentence:
I feel happy when . . .
I feel sad when . . .
I feel angry when . . .
I feel silly when . . .
I feel surprised when . . .

9

What's for Lunch?

Imagine you could open your lunch box and find whatever you wanted inside. Draw a picture of what you would find. Then describe it in writing.

10

A New Friend

Tell about a time when you made a new friend. Where did you meet? What did you do? Describe what you liked about this person. Are you still friends now?

First Writing Prompts © 2010 by Pamela Chanko. Scholastic Teaching Resources

September

Family Facts

On the left side of your paper, list the people in your family. Write *is* next to each name. Then add words to tell something about each person. Examples: *Mommy is funny. Dad is a good cook.*

A Perfect Pet

Draw the perfect pet. It can be a pet you have or would like to have. It can also be an imaginary pet, like a dinosaur. Describe your pet, telling its name and what makes it perfect for you.

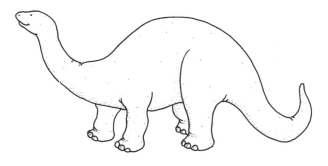

Cool Rules

Write a rule you think everyone at school should follow. It can be a rule the school already has, or one you would like to make. Tell why you think the rule is important.

P.S. I Love You

Write a note to someone you love, and tell this person what's happening at school. You can write about friends, activities, or whatever you think is important. Sign your name with *love* at the end.

Bedtime Stories

Name a story you like to read before bed. What is it about, and why do you like it? Tell what makes the story good for bedtime.

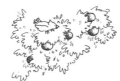 # September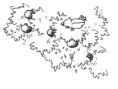

16

Fall Fun

Finish each sentence:
I know it's fall when . . .
The best thing about fall is . . .
Autumn leaves remind me of . . .
When it gets cooler outside, I . . .

17

On the Job

What job would you most like to do in the classroom? Write a letter to your teacher telling him or her why you would be great at it!

18

Teacher for a Day

Imagine a regular day in your classroom—only *you* are the teacher! Write a story to tell what happens and how it feels.

19

Letter-Perfect Poetry

Write your first initial four times down the left side of your paper. Write *is for* after the initial. Then write four good things that start with the letter. Example:
L is for lollipops, L is for laughing,
L is for learning, L is for love.

20

How I've Grown

Write three ways you have changed since you were a baby. Example:
I used to ride in a stroller, but now I walk by myself.

First Writing Prompts © 2010 by Pamela Chanko. Scholastic Teaching Resources

October

 21

Harvest Time

The fall harvest is in!
Finish these sentences:
Pumpkins are great for . . .
The best way to eat corn is . . .
An apple is ready to pick when . . .

 22

Scarecrow for a Day

Imagine you are a scarecrow.
Write a diary entry for one day,
telling what happens from morning
until night.

 23

Number Knowledge

Write about something you
learned in math. Tell how to do it,
step by step.

 24

Pumpkin Tales

In the fairy tale *Cinderella*, a magic
pumpkin turns into a coach to ride
in. Write your own story about a
special pumpkin.

 25

Red Leaf, Yellow Leaf

Write a dialogue between two
different-colored leaves. Make it
look like a play script. Example:
Red Leaf: I love changing color.
Yellow Leaf: Me, too!
Red Leaf: Are you afraid to fall down?
Yellow Leaf: Yes! Are you?

October

26
Out to Sea
Pretend you are going on a long ocean trip. Besides food and clothes, you can bring only ten items. Make a list. Then tell why you would take each thing with you.

27
Just Like Columbus
Imagine you are an explorer and your ship lands in a place you never even knew was there! Tell what you find there and what you will do in this new place.

28
Fighting Fire
Tell what you already know about firefighters. Then write three questions you would like to ask a firefighter.

29
Safety First!
How much do you know about fire safety? Finish these rules:
During a fire drill, you should . . .
If there is smoke, you should . . .
If you see matches, you should . . .

30
A Movie About You!
If a movie were made about your life, what would the title be? Who would be in it? Write a summary that tells the story.

First Writing Prompts © 2010 by Pamela Chanko. Scholastic Teaching Resources

October

 31

Meet My Machine

Pick any machine in your house and pretend you *are* the machine. Write at least one paragraph that tells how you feel. Example: *I'm a dishwasher. I get angry when you don't rinse the plates!*

 32

The Weekend Review

Write a review of your weekend as if it were a movie or a book. Give a summary of what happened. Tell the good parts and the bad parts. Then give it 1 to 4 stars to tell how much you liked it!

 33

Night and Day

Some animals, such as bats and owls, stay up all night and sleep all day. Other animals stay awake all day and sleep at night. Which kind of animal would you be, and why?

34

Face It!

What's the best kind of face for a jack-o'-lantern? Friendly? Funny? Frightening? Tell what you think and why.

35

Side by Side

Draw a line down the middle of your paper. On the left side, list things you like to do alone. On the right side, list things that are more fun to do with a friend.

October

 36

I Spy a Spider

Some spiders are named for how they look, like the wolf spider and the violin spider. Make up a new kind of spider. Draw it, describe it in words, and give it a name!

 37

That Black Cat!

Some people say it's bad luck if a black cat walks across your path. Do you agree? Give at least three reasons to back up your answer.

38

Hats Off to Halloween

Draw the perfect Halloween costume. Then describe your costume and tell why you like it.

39

Scary Tales

Tell about a time when you were really scared. What happened? How did things turn out?

 40

What's Inside?

Finish this haunted-house story:
I stood at the door. I was afraid to knock. But then the door creaked open and I saw . . .

14

November

Favorite Fashions

Draw your favorite thing to wear. Then write a description. Tell the color and texture. Tell where and when you wear it, and how it makes you feel.

Election News

Imagine that our country just elected a new president—you! Write a newspaper story telling how you won and what you will do as president.

Fun and Games

What's your favorite game to play? Explain the rules as if you were teaching someone who had never played before.

Sense It!

Across the top of your paper, write *See*, *Smell*, *Hear*, *Taste*, and *Touch*. Down the left side, write three places you like to go (for example, *beach*, *mall*, *zoo*). Then fill in the chart by writing what you can sense in each place.

Best Birthday

What was the best birthday you ever had? Tell what made it special: who was there, what you did, the gifts you got, and so on.

November

I've Got a Secret

What is something about you that might surprise people? Write an ad about yourself. Include a slogan about your secret surprise!
Example: *Beth studies seriously. But she's also seriously silly!*

Night School

Write a story about what happens at night when school is closed and everyone is at home. Use your imagination!

When I Grow Up

What do you want to be when you grow up? Write a schedule for a day on the job.
Example: *My Day as a Dancer*
7 AM: Do stretches
7:30 AM: Eat breakfast
8 AM: Go to ballet class

Window Watching

Look out a window for three minutes. Then turn away and write down everything you saw. Then look out the window again. How much did you remember?

Falling for Fall

Write a list of words that rhyme with *fall*. Then use your words to write a silly fall poem! Example:
I grew very tall.
My coat is too small.
I will shop at the mall
For a new coat for fall!

First Writing Prompts © 2010 by Pamela Chanko. Scholastic Teaching Resources

November

Yummy . . .

Describe your favorite food without naming it. Include its color, taste, texture, and anything else to help people guess the food.

. . . Yucky!

Describe a food you don't like. Give at least three reasons. Also tell about the last time you ate it. Would you ever try it again?

A Helping of Help

Thanksgiving is a lot of fun, but there's also lots of work to do. Tell how you help at the holiday.

Friends and Family

List the people you will spend Thanksgiving with this year. Write a sentence about each person describing them.

Write a Recipe

Write directions for a snack you know how to make. Example:

Bowl of Cereal

Ingredients:
* milk
* cereal

Directions:
1. Pour cereal in bowl.
2. Pour milk on cereal.

November

Thanks, World!

Write a thank-you note for all the things you are thankful for! Finish this note:

Dear World,
Thank you for . . .
Then sign your name at the end.

Guess Who's Coming to Thanksgiving Dinner

Write an invitation to Thanksgiving dinner. You can invite someone you know, someone famous, or a made-up character. Give the time, the place, and at least three reasons this guest should come!

The Mayflower Diaries

Imagine you are a Pilgrim child sailing to a new world. Divide your paper into four parts. In each section, write: *Today I . . .* Then write a journal entry for four different days.

Let's Talk Turkey

Imagine you are a turkey. This year, you want people to eat a different food on Thanksgiving. Design an ad to convince them!

Tell Me Why

Make up a story to explain why something in nature is the way it is. For example, why do giraffes have long necks? Or why do the stars shine at night? Use your imagination!

First Writing Prompts © 2010 by Pamela Chanko. Scholastic Teaching Resources

December

61

What the Snowflakes Said

What do snowflakes say as they fall from the sky? Draw some snowflakes and make speech bubbles to show their conversations.

62

Bear-y Special Dreams!

You know bears sleep in winter, but do they dream? Tell what you would dream about if you were a bear, and tell why.

63

The Missing Mitten

Write a story about a mitten that gets separated from its match. What happens to the mitten? Does it ever come back?

64

Winter Fun

There are many special things to do in winter, such as skiing and sledding. Describe your favorite winter activities and tell why you like them.

65

Top Ten Words

Make a list of your ten favorite words. Then write a sentence using each one.

December

66

Winter Is . . .

Write a poem about things that make you think of winter. Write the words *Winter is* five times down the left side of your paper. Then end each sentence with something wintry! Examples:

Winter is snowballs.
Winter is cocoa.

67

Loving Learning!

What is one subject you just love to learn about? Tell why you think it is interesting. Then tell what you know!

68

My Old Friend

Tell about an older person you spend time with. What do you do together? How is it different from spending time with friends your own age?

69

The Earth Stood Still

Imagine you could make time stand still for one minute. Nothing or nobody can move but you. What would you do in that minute?

70

Giving and Getting

An old saying goes, "It is better to give than to receive." Have you ever felt this way? Tell what this saying means to you.

December

71

Pass It On

Many holiday traditions are passed down in families. Tell about an old tradition in your family. Or, tell about a tradition you would like to start!

72

A Special Gift

Describe a holiday gift you have gotten that meant a lot to you. What was the gift, and who gave it to you? What made it special?

73

Decoration Station

Draw your favorite holiday decoration. It can be from home or school. Then describe it, and tell how it makes you feel inside.

74

Season's Greetings

Many people send cards during the holidays. Design a card with a message you could send to everyone you know.

75

Friends in Need

Sometimes people need extra help to have happy holidays. Write things you can do to cheer them up, such as give away warm clothes, cook good food, or give presents.

December

Light Up the Night!

Nights get longer in winter, but lights can help brighten them up! What kind of light is your favorite? Do you like candles, colored lights, or something else?

Gingerbread Me

If you were a gingerbread cookie, what would you look like? Draw a self-portrait and then write about your cookie.

Hooray for Holidays!

What holidays do you celebrate with your family? Name your favorite winter holiday and tell how you celebrate.

Time for Giving

Not all gifts cost money. You can give a hug or a helping hand for free! Make a list of other free holiday gifts you can give.

Wish You Were Here

Where would you like to go on winter vacation? Pretend you're there now. Write a postcard to a friend back home and tell about your trip!

January

Out With the Old, in With the New

List three ways you would like this year to be different from last year. How can you make each change happen?

How I Spent My Winter Vacation

Write what you did during winter vacation. Describe the holidays you celebrated, the places you went to, and the people you saw.

My Favorite Month

What is your favorite month of the year? Tell what happens in this month and why you like it.

Oh, Snow!

Tell what you know about snow. Where does it come from? When and where can you see it? What can you do with it?

Penguin Party!

Write a story about a group of penguins having fun together. Where do they live? What do they do?

January

Snow Day

Has it ever snowed so much that you got the day off from school? If yes, tell all about the day. If no, imagine what you would do and write about it!

Fair Is Fair

Tell about a time when you felt that you were treated unfairly. What happened? What did you do and how did you feel?

A Better Solution

Tell about a time when you and a friend were angry at each other. What happened? What could you do next time to make things better?

I Have a Dream

Martin Luther King, Jr., dreamed that all people would be treated equally. What idea do you have to make the world a better place?

Alike and Different

Draw a line down the middle of your paper. On the left side, write ways you and your friends are alike. On the right side, write ways you are different.

January

91

Snow Sculptures

Draw something you would like to make out of snow. Use your imagination! Then describe your creation and tell how to make it.

92

Shoot for the Stars

What would you like to be famous for? You could be anything from an inventor to a movie star! Write a story about your life in the spotlight.

93

New Kid on the Block

Tell about a time when you were new somewhere, such as a new town, school, or club. Then tell some ways people can make newcomers feel welcome.

94

Warming Up

What is your favorite way to stay warm? It could be eating soup, cuddling under blankets, or getting exercise! Tell how your activity warms you up and why you like it.

95

Up at the North Pole

Write a story that takes place in the Arctic. The characters can be animals, people, or both. Make sure to tell each thing that happens in order.

January

 96

Invent a Word

Make up your own word and decide what it means. Write the definition. Then use the word in a sentence.

 97

Now You See Me . . . Now You Don't

What would you do if you were invisible? What would your friends and family do when they found out? Write a story about your adventures.

 98

Beating the Blues

When you are sad, what do you do to cheer up? Tell what makes you feel better and why.

 **99**

It's in the Bag

What is in your backpack right now? List each thing, describe it, and tell how you use it.

100

What's Up With Grown-Ups?

Finish each sentence:

The thing I don't understand about grown-ups is . . .

The thing grown-ups don't understand about kids is . . .

The thing that would help kids and grown-ups understand each other is . . .

February

 101

Groundhogs in the Headlines

Write three possible newspaper headlines about Groundhog Day. Remember: A headline is short and to the point!

 102

The Melting Snowman

Pretend you're a snowman and the groundhog predicted that spring is on the way. Tell how you feel. What do you do?

103

My Lost Tooth

Tell the story of the first time you lost a tooth. If you haven't lost one yet, tell what you think will happen when you do!

 104

Tooth Fairy Tales

Imagine you could meet the Tooth Fairy. What would she look like? What magical powers would she have? Make up your own Tooth Fairy tale.

 105

Nobody's Perfect

Write about something a friend does that drives you crazy. Then tell something you might do to deal with the problem.

106

100 Days to 100 Years

About 100 days have gone by since school started this year. What will school be like when 100 *years* have gone by? What might be different? What do you think will stay the same?

107

I Wish I Had 100 . . .

Name something you would like to have 100 of, and tell why. Then tell about something it would *not* be good to have 100 of!

108

Words From the Heart

For Valentine's Day, you can get colored candy hearts with sayings like *Be Mine* and *Sweet Talk* on them. What words would you like to see on a candy heart? Make up five new sayings.

109

Valentine Rhymes

Make a list of words that rhyme with *blue*. Then use it to finish this Valentine's Day poem:
Roses are red, violets are blue . . .
Write the second line. End with a word on your list.

110

Complete the Compliments

Finish these compliments for people you love! Fill each blank on the left with a name. Fill each blank on the right with a word that completes the sentence. Example:
Todd is as smart as a scientist.
_____ *is as strong as* _____.
_____ *is as sweet as* _____.
_____ *is as funny as* _____.

111
Presidential Places

Many places in America are named after presidents. If you were president, what place would you want named after you? Tell where it is and what it's like.

112
Keep It Under Your Hat!

Abraham Lincoln kept notes to himself in his tall black hat. Write a note to yourself about something you need to remember. Then tell where you would keep it!

113
George, the First

George Washington was our country's first president. Do you think being first was easy or hard? Name something you'd like to be first to do. Tell what you'd enjoy and what might be hard.

114
Dear Mr. President

List five things you want to tell the president and five questions you want to ask. Then write a letter including the two most important things from each list.

115
The President's House

The White House has 132 rooms, 35 bathrooms, and even a bowling alley! Design the house you'd have as president. Label each room and tell its use. Make your house any color you like!

February

Apply Yourself!

Write a job description for being a good friend. Finish these lines:
Should be good at . . .
Should always try to . . .
Should almost never . . .
Then read your sentences and tell if you would get the job!

Trading Places

If you could trade places with anyone in the world, who would you choose and why? Tell how your life would be different.

A Lesson Learned

Difficult experiences can make you stronger—and smarter. Write about a hard time that taught you something. What happened, and what did you learn?

Make 'Em Laugh

Do you have a favorite joke to tell? Write it down. Try to use the same words you would use if you were telling it out loud.

Leap Day

February 29 is only on the calendar every four years. In other years, this day does not happen! Write a story that takes place on Leap Day.

First Writing Prompts © 2010 by Pamela Chanko. Scholastic Teaching Resources

March

121

Let's Go Fly a Kite

Design a kite you would like to fly. Draw it and describe each part. Then tell a story about what happens when you fly your kite for the first time.

122

Locked in the Library

What would happen if someone was so busy reading she didn't see the library was closing? Write a story about the overnight adventure. Use your imagination!

123

Read Across America

Divide your paper into four parts and label the sections *City, Forest, Farm,* and *Ocean.* Write titles of stories you know that take place in each setting.

124

Author, Author!

What author would you most like to meet? Explain why. Then write at least five questions you would ask the author.

125

Windy Weather

Write a poem about what happens in the wind. For each line, name a group of things and an action.
Example:
Kites fly.
Hair blows.
Trees bend.
Boats sail.

March

Do You Read Me?

Write at least three reasons it's important to learn to read. Finish this sentence in three ways: *If you couldn't read . . .* Examples:
you wouldn't understand signs.
you'd buy the wrong groceries.
you couldn't follow directions.

What a Whopper!

A *tall tale* is an unbelievable story with wacky details that are told as if they were true. Write a tall tale titled *Why I Was Late to School Today*. Make up the craziest excuses you can!

I Did It!

Name something you did in the past week that made you feel proud. Then write an e-mail to the person you want to tell most!

Food Fight!

Should schools have snack and soda machines? Divide your paper in half and label the sides *Yes* and *No*. Write a good argument for each side. Then turn over the paper and tell which side you agree with.

Wonder Woman

Write about a woman you admire. She can be someone from history, someone famous, or a woman you know. Describe the things about her you admire.

March

Leapin' Leprechauns!

Imagine a group of leprechauns snuck into the classroom one night. Write a news story telling what you saw the next morning!

Rainbow Wishes

A legend says that if you go to the end of the rainbow, you might find a pot of gold. Tell a story about going to the end of a rainbow and finding a surprise.

Lots of Luck!

Some people have a good-luck charm, such as a lucky penny or a special hat. Do you have any good-luck charms? Do you believe they work? Explain why.

Backwards Day

Imagine a day when everything happens backwards. Tell each thing you do in that order! Example: *First, I turn out the light. Then I put on my pajamas. Next, I eat dinner . . .*

Awesome Artwork

What is your favorite way to make art? Do you like working with clay? Painting? Drawing? Describe how you make your art and why you enjoy it.

March

Music to My Ears

Name a musical instrument you know how to play or would like to learn. What does it sound like? Why did you choose it?

Build a Meal

Design a perfect meal. Your meal should be good *and* good for you. Draw each food. Then tell how it tastes and why it is healthy.

Loud and Soft

What do you like most: noisy times, quiet times, or some of each? Give reasons and examples.

House Rules

If you were the head of your house, what changes would you make at home? What would you want to stay the same?

From Lion to Lamb

A saying goes, "March comes in like a lion and goes out like a lamb." First, tell what you think the saying means. Then tell if you think it's true where you live.

April

141

April Fool's!

Do you like playing April Fool's tricks? How about when people play them on you? Explain your feelings with examples.

142

Stormy Weather

You've probably heard the saying, "It's raining cats and dogs." What if it could rain any two things you wanted? Tell what you would choose and why.

143

Poetry for Me

Describe a poem you like. Tell what it's about, how it sounds, and how it makes you feel.

144

Circle of Life

Pretend you're a butterfly and tell your life story. Describe hatching from the egg, being a caterpillar, spinning a chrysalis, and becoming a butterfly.

145

Spring Sound Poem

Copy this line three times:

_____ *goes the* _____.

Fill the blanks with a sound and what makes it. Example:
Cheep goes the *bird*.
Croak goes the *frog*.
Splash goes the *puddle*.

April

146

To Tell the Truth

Is it always right to tell the truth, no matter what? Give examples with your opinion.

147

The Best Babysitter

Write a list of traits every good babysitter should have. Then tell if you would make a good babysitter and why.

148

Color My World

Name your favorite color. Then make a list including:

* things that are that color
* things you wish were that color
* ways that color makes you feel

149

Science Nonfiction

Scientists can study weather, plants, computers, animals, and many other things. If you were a scientist, what would you study? Why?

150

An Egg-citing Surprise!

Write a story about an egg that hatches something surprising. Give your story an exciting beginning. Example: *At last, a tapping sound came from inside the egg. Everyone watched and waited. Finally, there was a loud crack, and . . .*

April

151

Make an Earth Day Wish

What wish do you have for our world? Would you like cleaner air? More trees? Better places for animals to live? Tell how you can help make your wish come true.

152

Recycling Rules!

Explain how you recycle at school and at home. What rules do you follow in each place?

153

Ask Mother Nature

Imagine you could interview Mother Nature. Write five questions you would ask. Then choose one question and write what her answer might be.

154

Trash to Treasure

Design an invention made only from things you recycle. Draw your creation and then explain how it works.

155

Out of This World!

Invent your own planet and then write a story about it! What does your planet look like? What or who lives there? How is it different from Earth?

April

156

Design a Tree

Lots of things grow on trees. What if you could plant a tree to grow anything you wanted? Draw a picture of your tree and then describe it.

157

They're Playing My Song

Describe your favorite song and tell what you like about it. Is it fast or slow? What do the words say? How do you feel when you hear it?

158

All in a Day's Work

What jobs do the grown-ups in your family do? Tell about one family member's job. How is the work different from schoolwork? How is it the same?

159

Good Advice

What advice would you give to a child your age who just moved to your neighborhood? Give your new neighbor tips about school, places to go, and things to do.

160

History Time Travel

What times in history have you learned about in social studies? Imagine you can go back in time, and tell what year you would visit. What would you do? How would it be different from today?

First Writing Prompts © 2010 by Pamela Chanko. Scholastic Teaching Resources

May

161 Growing, Growing, Gone!

Tell about a vegetable you have grown or would like to grow in a garden. Tell each step in order, from planting it to eating it!

162 Springing Into Action

List five to ten things you can see in your neighborhood in spring, but not in winter. Then make a check mark next to the things you've seen so far this spring!

163 Zoo Interview

Imagine that you could ask any animal a question and understand the answer. What animal would you choose, and what would you ask? What might the answer be?

164 Build a Bloom!

Invent a new kind of flower. It can look or smell like anything you want. Draw your flower. Then write a paragraph to describe it.

165 Leaving the Nest

Write a story about a baby bird who is afraid of flying. What does the bird do? How does it feel? Give your story a beginning, middle, and end.

166

Mom's the Word

The dictionary says that *mom* is a short word for "mother." But what does the word mean to you? Finish this sentence at least three different ways:

A mom is . . .

167

All About My Mother

How much do you know about your mom? Write one paragraph about her life before you were born, and one about her life after. If the first paragraph is short, interview your mom to find out more!

168

What's in a Name?

If you could change your name to anything, what would you change it to? Why?

169

Go Buggy!

What is your favorite kind of insect? Tell everything you know about it, such as what it eats, where it lives, and how it grows.

170

Pack for a Picnic

Write a list of things to bring on a picnic. Then describe the place where you would have your picnic and the people you would invite along!

May

 171

The Best Books

What is your favorite kind of book to read? Do you like true stories? Fairy tales? Mysteries? Name your favorite kind of book and tell why you like it.

 172

Then What Happened?

Choose a story you like. Then write a new story to tell what happens after the first one ends.

 173

Character Improvement

Not every story character is someone you'd like in real life. Describe a character you don't like. What could the author do to make you like him or her more?

 174

Setting the Scene

If you could spend a day in the setting of any story, what setting would you visit? What would you do there? Describe your day.

 175

Tempting Titles

A good title can make you want to read the whole book. Write three good titles for children's books. Then pick your favorite and write a short summary, telling what the book is about.

May

176

The Me Book

Design a cover for a book that's all about you! Include a title and a picture. Then write an ad for the book that will make people want to read it.

177

Tongue-Twister Fun

Make a list of words that start with the same sound as your name. Then write a tongue twister about yourself! Example:
Tina turns ten tiny toys on the table at tea time.

178

Super Science

Tell about something you learned in science that you think is interesting. You can draw a picture or diagram if it will help you explain what you learned.

179

To Bee or Not to Bee

Some people don't like bees. But bees are very helpful insects. Write at least one reason to like bees. Then write one reason people might not like them.

180

Help the Animals

Make a list of ways that people can be kind to animals. You can include pets and wild animals. Circle something on your list that you can start doing right now. Then go out and do it!

June
and Beyond

181

Making the Grade

Tell students who will be entering your grade next year what to expect. What is the most important thing they will learn?

182

School Memories

List at least five things you would put in a time capsule to remember this year at school. Tell what each thing reminds you of and why it's important to remember.

183

Planning Ahead

What will you do during summer vacation? Describe places you will go, things you will do, and people you will see.

184

Hot and Cold

Some people love hot weather, others like it cold, and some like a little of each! Which type of person are you? Explain why.

185

And the Award Goes to . . .

Some moments are so special, they deserve an award! Tell what would get each of these awards:

- *Funniest Moment of the Year*
- *Weirdest Moment of the Year*
- *Saddest Moment of the Year*
- *Proudest Moment of the Year*

June and Beyond

186

A Day for Dad

Some dads like reading. Others like running. Describe what you think your dad's idea of a perfect Father's Day would be.

187

Father's Day Funnies

What's the most fun you've ever had with your dad? Make a comic strip to tell about it. Draw pictures in order to show what happened. Write speech bubbles to help you tell the story.

188

The Perfect Getaway!

Imagine the perfect vacation. Write a short magazine article to describe the place and what you can do there.

189

Castle Contest

Some beaches hold sand castle contests. Draw a sand castle that you think could win a contest. Then write why it would win.

190

Under Starry Skies

What do you think about when you look at the stars? Do you make wishes? See pictures in the sky? Imagine going to space? Express your thoughts!

First Writing Prompts © 2010 by Pamela Chanko. Scholastic Teaching Resources

June
and Beyond

191

Under the Sea

Write a story that takes place underwater. Your story can be about animals, people, or both. Give the characters a problem they can solve by the end.

192

My Independence Day

Independence means doing things without anyone's help. Write about a day when you did something by yourself for the first time, such as crossing the street or riding a bike. How did it feel?

193

Kaboom!

Have you ever seen a fireworks show? Describe what you saw and heard. If you haven't seen fireworks, use your imagination!

194

We All Scream for Ice Cream!

Invent a new flavor of ice cream. Then design an ad that will make people want to try it. Include words and pictures.

195

Summer Safety

Divide your paper in half. On the left side, write a list of summer activities. On the right side, write a safety rule for each one. Example: *Going on a sailboat / Always wear a life vest.*

June
and Beyond

196

A Wild Ride

Draw an exciting ride at a fair or amusement park. It can be a ride you have taken, or one you invent. Then describe the ride, including how it moves and how it feels to ride it!

197

Campfire Stories

Write a funny story that takes place at camp. Your story can be true or made up, as long as it makes you laugh!

198

Old Friends, New Friends

Write one paragraph that explains what's good about having old friends. Then write a paragraph that explains what's good about making new ones.

199

My Robot

If you could invent a robot or machine to do any job, what would it do? Why?

200

Summer From Start to Finish

Finish these sentences:
When summer starts, I . . .
The best part of summer is . . .
Summer is almost over when . . .
At the end of the summer . . .

Name _____

Name _____

First Writing Prompts © 2010 by Pamela Chanko. Scholastic Teaching Resources